D1498175

A GEHENNA FACSIMILE

SOME CONSIDERATIONS ON THE KEEPING OF NEGROES

1754

CONSIDERATIONS ON KEEPING NEGROES

1762

JOHN WOOLMAN 1720-1772

GROSSMAN PUBLISHERS · A DIVISION OF THE VIKING PRESS

Published in 1976 by Grossman Publishers
625 Madison Avenue, New York, N.Y. 10022
Published simultaneously in Canada by
The Macmillan Company of Canada Limited
Printed in U.S.A.

Library of Congress Cataloging in Publication Data
Woolman, John, 1720–1772.
    Some considerations on the keeping of Negroes, 1754.
    Reprint of the 1970 ed. published by the Gehenna
Press, Northampton, which was issued as no. 2 of: The
Gehenna tracts.
1. Slavery. I. Title. II. Title: Considerations
on the keeping of Negroes.
HT871.W6 1976   301.44'93   75-40466
ISBN 0-670-23892-9

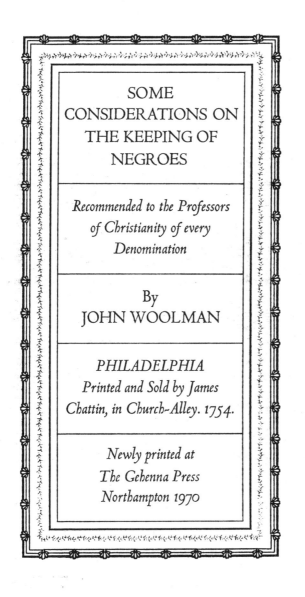

SOME CONSIDERATIONS ON THE KEEPING OF NEGROES

Recommended to the Professors of Christianity of every Denomination

By
JOHN WOOLMAN

PHILADELPHIA
Printed and Sold by James Chattin, in Church-Alley. 1754.

Newly printed at
The Gehenna Press
Northampton 1970

INTRODUCTION

Customs *generally approved, and* Opinions *received by Youth from their Superiors, become like the natural Produce of a Soil, especially when they are suited to favourite Inclinations: But as the Judgments of God are without Partiality, by which the State of the Soul must be tried, it would be the highest Wisdom to forego Customs and popular Opinions, and try the Treasures of the Soul by the infallible Standard* Truth.

Natural Affection needs a careful Examination: Operating upon us in a soft Manner, it kindles Desires of Love and Tenderness, and there is Danger of taking it for something higher. To me it appears an Instinct like that which inferior Creatures have; each of them, we see, by the Ties of Nature, love Self *best; that which is a Part of* Self *they love by the same Tie or Instinct. In them it in some Measure does the Offices of Reason, by which, among other Things, they watchfully keep, and orderly feed their helpless Offspring. Thus* Natural Affection *appears to be a Branch of* Self-love, *good in the Animal Race, in us likewise, with proper Limitations; but otherwise is productive of Evil, by exciting Desires to promote some by Means prejudicial to others.*

Our Blessed Saviour seems to give a Check to this irregular Fondness in Nature, and, at the same Time, a President for us: Who is my Mother, and who are my Brethren? *Thereby intimating, that the earthly Ties of Relationship, are, comparatively, inconsiderable to such who, thro' a steady Course of Obedience, have come to the happy Experience of the Spirit* of God bearing witness with their Spirits that they are his Children:—And he stretched forth his Hands towards his Disciples, and said, Behold my Mother and my Brethren: For whosoever shall do the Will of my Father which is in Heaven [*arrives at the more noble Part of true Relationship*] the same is my Brother, and Sister, and Mother, Mat. xii. 48.

This Doctrine agrees well with a State truly compleat, where Love *necessarily operates according to the Agreeableness of Things on Principles unalterable and in themselves perfect.*

If endeavouring to have my Children eminent amongst Men after my Death, be that which no Reasons grounded on those Principles can be brought to support; then to be temperate in my Pursuit after Gain, and to keep always within the Bounds of those Principles, is an indispensable Duty, and to depart from it, a dark unfruitful Toil.

In our present Condition, to love *our Children is needful; but except this* Love *proceeds from the true heavenly Principle which sees beyond earthly Treasures, it will rather be injurious than of any real Advantage to them; Where the Fountain is corrupt, the Streams must necessarily be impure.*

That important Injunction of our Saviour, Mat. vi. 33. *with the Promise annexed, contains a short but comprehensive View of our Duty and Happiness:—If then the Business of Mankind in this Life, is, to first seek another; if this cannot be done, but by attending to the Means; if a Summary of the Means is,* Not to do that to another which, in like Circumstances, we would not have done unto us, *then these are Points of Moment, and worthy of our most serious Consideration.*

What I write on this Subject is with Reluctance, and the Hints given are in as general Terms as my Concern would allow: I know it is a Point about which in all its Branches Men that appear to aim well are not generally agreed, and for that Reason I chose to avoid being very particular:—If I may happily have let drop any Thing that may excite such as are concerned in the Practice to a close Thinking on the Subject treated of, the Candid amongst them may easily do the Subject such further Justice, as, on an impartial Enquiry, it may appear to deserve; and such an Enquiry I would earnestly recommend.

SOME
CONSIDERATIONS
On the KEEPING of
NEGROES.

Forasmuch as ye did it to the least of these my Brethren,
ye did it unto me, Mat. xxv. 40.

As Many Times there are different Motives to the
same Actions; and one does that from a generous
Heart, which another does for selfish Ends:—The
like may be said in this Case.

There are various Circumstances amongst them
that keep *Negroes,* and different Ways by which they
fall under their Care; and, I doubt not, there are
many well disposed Persons amongst them who
desire rather to manage wisely and justly in this
difficult Matter, than to make Gain of it.

But the general Disadvantage which these poor
Africans lie under in an enlight'ned Christian Country,
having often fill'd me with real Sadness, and been
like undigested Matter on my Mind, I now think it
my Duty, through Divine Aid, to offer some
Thoughts thereon to the Consideration of others.

When we remember that all Nations are of one
Blood, *Gen.* iii. 20. that in this World we are but
Sojourners, that we are subject to the like Afflictions
and Infirmities of Body, the like Disorders and
Frailties in Mind, the like Temptations, the same

Death, and the same Judgment, and, that the Alwise Being is Judge and Lord over us all, it seems to raise an Idea of a general Brotherhood, and a Disposition easy to be touched with a Feeling of each others Afflictions: But when we forget those Things, and look chiefly at our outward Circumstances, in this and some Ages past, constantly retaining in our Minds the Distinction betwixt us and them, with respect to our Knowledge and Improvement in Things divine, natural and artificial, our Breasts being apt to be filled with fond Notions of Superiority, there is Danger of erring in our Conduct toward them.

We allow them to be of the same Species with ourselves, the Odds is, we are in a higher Station, and enjoy greater Favours than they: And when it is thus, that our heavenly Father endoweth some of his Children with distinguished Gifts, they are intended for good Ends; but if those thus gifted are thereby lifted up above their Brethren, not considering themselves as Debtors to the Weak, nor behaving themselves as faithful Stewards, none who judge impartially can suppose them free from Ingratitude.

When a People dwell under the liberal Distribution of Favours from Heaven, it behoves them carefully to inspect their Ways, and consider the Purposes for which those Favours were bestowed, lest, through

Forgetfulness of God, and Misusing his Gifts, they incur his heavy Displeasure, whose Judgments are just and equal, who exalteth and humbleth to the Dust as he seeth meet.

It appears by Holy Record that Men under high Favours have been apt to err in their Opinions concerning others. Thus *Israel*, according to the Description of the Prophet, *Isai.* lxv. 5. when exceedingly corrupted and degenerated, yet remembered they were the chosen People of God and could say, *Stand by thyself, come not near me, for I am holier than thou.* That this was no chance Language, but their common Opinion of other People, more fully appears by considering the Circumstances which attended when God was beginning to fulfil his precious Promises concerning the Gathering of the *Gentiles*.

The Most High, in a Vision, undeceived *Peter*, first prepared his Heart to believe; and, at the House of *Cornelius*, shewed him of a Certainty that God was no Respector of Persons.

The Effusion of the Holy Ghost upon a People with whom they, the *Jewish* Christians, would not so much as eat, was strange to them: All they of the Circumcision were astonished to see it; and the Apostles and Brethren of *Judea* contended with *Peter* about it, till he, having rehearsed the whole Matter, and fully shewn that the Father's Love was unlimited, they are thereat struck with Admiration, and cry out; *Then hath God also to the* Gentiles *granted Repentance unto Life!*

The Opinion of peculiar Favours being confined to them, was deeply rooted, or else the above Instance had been less strange to them, for these Reasons: *First,* They were generally acquainted with the Writings of the Prophets, by whom this Time was repeatedly spoken of, and pointed at. *Secondly,* Our Blessed Lord shortly before expressly said, *I have other Sheep, not of this Fold, them also must I bring,* &c. *Lastly,* His Words to them after his Resurrection, at the very Time of his Ascension, *Ye shall be Witnesses to me, not only in* Jerusalem, Judea, *and* Samaria, *but to the uttermost Parts of the Earth.*

Those concurring Circumstances, one would think, might have raised a strong Expectation of seeing such a Time; yet, when it came, it proved Matter of Offence and Astonishment.

To consider Mankind otherwise than Brethren, to think Favours are peculiar to one Nation, and exclude others, plainly supposes a Darkness in the Understanding: For as God's Love is universal, so where the Mind is sufficiently influenced by it, it begets a Likeness of itself, and the Heart is enlarged towards all Men. Again, to conclude a People froward, perverse, and worse by Nature than others (who ungratefully receive Favours, and apply them to bad Ends) this will excite a Behaviour toward them unbecoming the Excellence of true Religion.

To prevent such Error, let us calmly consider their Circumstance; and, the better to do it, make their Case ours. Suppose, then, that our Ancestors and we had been exposed to constant Servitude in the more servile and inferior Employments of Life; that we had been destitute of the Help of Reading and good Company; that amongst ourselves we had had few wise and pious Instructors; that the Religious amongst our Superiors seldom took Notice of us; that while others, in Ease, have plentifully heap'd up the Fruit of our Labour, we had receiv'd barely enough to relieve Nature, and being wholly at the Command of others, had generally been treated as a contemptible, ignorant Part of Mankind: Should we, in that Case, be less abject than they now are? Again, If Oppression be so hard to bear, that a wise Man is made mad by it, *Eccl*. vii. 7. then a Series of those Things altering the Behaviour and Manners of a People, is what may reasonably be expected.

When our Property is taken contrary to our Mind, by Means appearing to us unjust, it is only through divine Influence, and the Enlargement of Heart

14

from thence proceeding, that we can love our reputed Oppressors: If the *Negroes* fall short in this, an uneasy, if not a disconsolate Disposition, will be awak'ned, and remain like Seeds in their Minds, producing Sloth and many other Habits appearing odious to us, with which being free Men, they, perhaps, had not been chargeable. These, and other Circumstances, rightly considered, will lessen that too great Disparity, which some make between us and them.

Integrity of Heart hath appeared in some of them; so that if we continue in the Word of Christ [previous to Discipleship, *John* viii. 31.] and our Conduct towards them be seasoned with his Love, we may hope to see the good Effect of it: The which, in a good Degree, is the Case with some into whose Hands they have fallen: But that too many treat them otherwise, not seeming concious of any Neglect, is, alas! too evident.

When *Self-love* presides in our Minds, our Opinions are bias'd in our own Favour; in this Condition, being concerned with a People so situated, that they have no Voice to plead their own Cause, there's Danger of using ourselves to an undisturbed Partiality, till, by long Custom, the Mind becomes reconciled with it, and the Judgment itself infected.

To humbly apply to God for Wisdom, that we may

thereby be enabled to see Things as they are, and ought to be, is very needful; hereby the hidden Things of Darkness may be brought to light, and the Judgment made clear: We shall then consider Mankind as Brethren: Though different Degrees and a Variety of Qualifications and Abilities, one dependant on another, be admitted, yet high Thoughts will be laid aside, and all Men treated as becometh the Sons of one Father, agreeable to the Doctrine of Christ Jesus.

"He hath laid down the best Criterion, by which "Mankind ought to judge of their own Conduct, "and others judge for them of theirs, one towards "another, *viz. Whatsoever ye would that Men should do unto* "*you, do ye even so to them.* I take it, that all Men "by Nature, are equally entituled to the Equity of "this Rule, and under the indispensable Obligations "of it. One Man ought not to look upon another "Man, or Society of Men, as so far beneath him, "but that he should put himself in their Place, in all "his Actions towards them, and bring all to this "Test, *viz.* How should I approve of this Conduct, "were I in their Circumstance and they in mine? *A. Arscot's* Considerations, Part III. Fol. 107.

This Doctrine being of a moral unchangeable Nature, hath been likewise inculcated in the former Dispensation; *If a Stranger sojourn with thee in your Land, ye shall not vex him; but the Stranger that dwelleth with you, shall be as One born amongst you, and thou shalt love him as thyself.* Lev. xix. 33, 34. Had these People come voluntarily and dwelt amongst us, to have called them Strangers would be proper; and their being brought by Force, with Regret, and a languishing Mind, may well raise Compassion in a Heart rightly disposed: But there is Nothing in such Treatment, which upon a wise and judicious Consideration, will any Ways lessen their Right of being treated as Strangers. If the Treatment which many of them meet with, be rightly examined and compared with those Precepts, *Thou shalt not vex him nor oppress him; he shall be as one born amongst you, and thou shalt love him as thyself,* Lev. xix. 33. Deut. xxvii. 19. there will appear an important Difference betwixt them.

It may be objected there is Cost of Purchase, and Risque of their Lives to them who possess 'em, and therefore needful that they make the best Use of their Time: In a Practice just and reasonable, such Objections may have Weight; but if the Work be wrong from the Beginning, there's little or no Force in them. If I purchase a Man who hath never forfeited his Liberty, the natural Right of Freedom is in him; and shall I keep him and his Posterity in Servitude and Ignorance? "How should I approve of "this Conduct, were I in his Circumstances, and "he in mine? It may be thought, that to treat them as we would willingly be treated, our Gain by them would be inconsiderable: And it were, in divers Respects, better that there were none in our Country.

We may further consider, that they are now amongst us, and those of our Nation the Cause of their being here; that whatsoever Difficulty accrues thereon, we are justly chargeable with, and to bear all Inconveniences attending it, with a serious and weighty Concern of Mind to do our Duty by them, is the best we can do. To seek a Remedy by continuing the Oppression, because we have Power to do it, and see others do it, will, I apprehend, not be doing as we would be done by.

How deeply soever Men are involved in the most exquisite Difficulties, Sincerity of Heart, and upright Walking before God, freely submitting to his Providence, is the most sure Remedy: He only is able to relieve, not only Persons, but Nations, in their greatest Calamities.

David, in a great Strait, when the Sense of his past Error, and the full Expectation of an impending Calamity, as the Reward of it, were united to the agravating his Distress, after some Deliberation, saith, *Let me fall now into the Hands of the Lord, for very great are his Mercies; let me not fall into the Hand of Man,* 1 Chron. xxi. 13.

To act continually with Integrity of Heart, above all narrow or selfish Motives, is a sure Token of our being Partakers of that Salvation which *God hath appointed for Walls and Bulwarks*, Isa. v. 26. Rom. xv. 8. and is, beyond all Contradiction, a more happy Situation than can ever be promised by the utmost Reach of Art and Power united, not proceeding from heavenly Wisdom.

A Supply to Nature's lawful Wants, joined with a peaceful, humble Mind, is the truest Happiness in this Life; and if here we arrive to this, and remain to walk in the Path of the Just, our Case will be truly happy: And though herein we may part with, or miss of some glaring Shews of Riches, and leave our Children little else but wise Instructions, a good Example, and the Knowledge of some honest Employment, these, with the Blessing of Providence, are sufficient for their Happiness, and are more likely to prove so, than laying up Treasures for them, which are often rather a Snare, than any real Benefit; especially to them, who, instead of being exampled to Temperance, are in all Things taught to prefer the getting of Riches, and to eye the temporal Distinctions they give, as the principal Business of this Life. These readily overlook the true Happiness of Man, as it results from the Enjoyment of all Things in the Fear of God, and, miserably substituting an inferior Good, dangerous in the Acquiring, and uncertain in the Fruition, they are subject to many Disappointments, and every Sweet carries its Sting.

It is the Conclusion of our blessed Lord and his Apostles, as appears by their Lives and Doctrines, that the highest Delights of Sense, or most pleasing Objects visible, ought ever to be accounted infinitely inferior to that real intellectual Happiness suited to Man in his primitive Innocence, and now to be found in true Renovation of Mind; and that the Comforts of our present Life, the Things most grateful to us, ought always to be receiv'd with Temperance, and never made the chief Objects of our Desire, Hope, or Love: But that our whole Heart and Affections be principally looking to that *City which hath Foundations, whose Maker and Builder is God.* Did we so improve the Gifts bestowed on us, that our Children might have an Education suited to these Doctrines, and our Example to confirm it, we might rejoice in Hopes of their being Heirs of an Inheritance incorruptible.

This Inheritance, as Christians, we esteem the most valuable; and how then can we fail to desire it for our Children? O that we were consistent with ourselves, in pursuing Means necessary to obtain it!

It appears, by Experience, that where Children are

educated in Fulness, Ease and Idleness, evil Habits are more prevalent, than in common amongst such who are prudently employed in the necessary Affairs of Life: And if Children are not only educated in the Way of so great Temptation, but have also the Opportunity of lording it over their Fellow Creatures, and being Masters of Men in their Childhood, how can we hope otherwise than that their tender Minds will be possessed with Thoughts too high for them? Which, by Continuance, gaining Strength, will prove, like a slow Current, gradually separating them from [or keeping from Acquaintance with] that Humility and Meekness in which alone lasting Happiness can be enjoyed.

Man is born to labour, and Experience abundantly sheweth, that it is for our Good: But where the Powerful lay the Burthen on the Inferior, without affording a Christian Education, and suitable Opportunity of improving the Mind, and a Treatment which we, in their Case, should approve, that themselves may live at Ease, and fare sumptuously, and lay up Riches for their Posterity, this seems to contradict the Design of Providence, and, I doubt, is sometimes the Effect of a perverted Mind: For while the Life of one is made grievous by the Rigour of another, it entails Misery on both.

Amongst the manifold Works of Providence,

displayed in the different Ages of the World, these which follow [with many others] may afford Instruction.

Abraham was called of God to leave his Country and Kindred, to sojourn amongst Strangers: Through Famine, and Danger of Death, he was forced to flee from one Kingdom to another: He, at length, not only had Assurance of being the Father of many Nations, but became a mighty Prince, *Gen.* xxiii. 6.

Remarkable was the Dealings of God with *Jacob* in a low Estate, the just Sense he retained of them after his Advancement, appears by his Words; *I am not worthy of the Least of all thy Mercies,* Gen. xxxii. 10. xlviii. 15.

The numerous Afflictions of *Joseph*, are very singular; the particular Providence of God therein, no less manifest: He, at length, became Governor of *Egypt*, and famous for Wisdom and Virtue.

The Series of Troubles *David* passed through, few amongst us are ignorant of; and yet he afterwards became as one of the great Men of the Earth.

Some Evidences of the Divine Wisdom appears in those Things, in that such who are intended for high Stations, have first been very low and dejected, that Truth might be sealed on their Hearts, and that the Characters there imprinted by Bitterness and Adversity, might in after Years remain, suggesting compassionate Ideas, and, in their Prosperity, quicken their Regard to those in the like Condition: Which yet further appears in the Case of *Israel*: They were well acquainted with grievous Sufferings, a long and rigorous Servitude, then, through many notable Events, were made Chief amongst the Nations: To them we find a Repetition of Precepts to the Purpose abovesaid: Though, for Ends agreeable to infinite Wisdom, they were chose as a peculiar People for a Time; yet the Most High acquaints them, that his Love is not confined, but extends to the Stranger; and, to excite their Compassion, reminds them of Times past, *Ye were Strangers in the Land of* Egypt, Deut. x. 19. Again, *Thou shalt not oppress a Stranger, for ye know the Heart of a Stranger, seeing ye were Strangers in the Land of* Egypt, Exod. xxiii. 9.

If we call to Mind our Beginning, some of us may find a Time, wherein our Fathers were under Afflictions, Reproaches, and manifold Sufferings.

Respecting our Progress in this Land, the Time is short since our Beginning was small and Number few, compared with the native Inhabitants. He that sleeps not by Day nor Night, hath watched over us, and kept us as the Apple of his Eye. His Almighty Arm hath been round about us, and saved us from Dangers.

The Wilderness and solitary Desarts in which our Fathers passed the Days of their Pilgrimage, are now turned into pleasant Fields; the Natives are gone from before us, and we established peaceably in the Possession of the Land, enjoying our civil and religious Liberties; and, while many Parts of the World have groaned under the heavy Calamities of War, our Habitation remains quiet, and our Land fruitful.

When we trace back the Steps we have trodden, and see how the Lord hath opened a Way in the Wilderness for us, to the Wise it will easily appear, that all this was not done to be buried in Oblivion; but to prepare a People for more fruitful Returns, and the Remembrance thereof, ought to humble us in Prosperity, and excite in us a Christian Benevolence towards our Inferiors.

If we do not consider these Things aright, but, through a stupid Indolence, conceive Views of Interest, separate from the general Good of the great Brotherhood, and, in Pursuance thereof, treat our Inferiors with Rigour, to increase our Wealth, and gain Riches for our Children, what then shall we do, when God riseth up, and when he visiteth, what shall we Answer him? Did not he that made Us, make Them, and *Did not one Fashion us in the Womb?* Job. xxxi. 14, 15.

To our great Master we stand or fall, to judge or condemn is most suitable to his Wisdom and Authority; my Inclination is to persuade, and intreat, and simply give Hints of my Way of Thinking.

If the Christian Religion be considered, both respecting its Doctrines, and the happy Influence which it hath on the Minds and Manners of all real Christians, it looks reasonable to think, that the miraculous Manifestation thereof to the World, is a Kindness beyond Expression.

Are we the People thus favoured? Are we they whose Minds are opened, influenced, and govern'd by the Spirit of Christ, and thereby made Sons of God? Is it not a fair Conclusion, that we, like our heavenly Father, ought, in our Degree, to be active in the same great Cause, of the Eternal Happiness of, at least, our whole Families, and more, if thereto capacitated?

If we, by the Operation of the Spirit of Christ, become Heirs with him in the Kingdom of his Father, and are redeemed from the alluring counterfeit Joys of this World, and the Joy of Christ remain in us, to suppose that One remaining in this happy Condition, can for the Sake of earthly Riches, not only deprive his Fellow Creatures of the Sweetness of Freedom [which, rightly used, is one of the greatest temporal Blessings] but therewith neglect using proper Means, for their Acquaintance with the Holy Scriptures, and the Advantage of true Religion, seems, at least, a Contradiction to Reason.

Whoever rightly advocates the Cause of some, thereby promotes the Good of all. The State of Mankind was harmonious in the Beginning, and tho' Sin hath introduced Discord, yet, through the wonderful Love of God, in Christ Jesus our Lord, the Way is open for our Redemption, and Means appointed to restore us to primitive Harmony. That if one suffer, by the Unfaithfulness of another, the Mind, the most noble Part of him that occasions the Discord, is thereby alienated from its true and real Happiness.

Our Duty and Interest is inseparably united, and when we neglect or misuse our Talents, we necessarily depart from the heavenly Fellowship, and are in the Way to the greatest of Evils.

Therefore, to examine and prove ourselves, to find what Harmony the Power presiding in us bears with the Divine Nature, is a Duty not more incumbent and necessary, than it would be beneficial.

In Holy Writ the Divine Being saith of himself, *I am the Lord, which exercise Loving Kindness, Judgment and Righteousness in the Earth; for in these Things I delight, saith the Lord,* Jer. ix. 24. Again, speaking in the Way of Man, to shew his Compassion to *Israel,* whose Wickedness had occasioned a Calamity, and then being humbled under it, it is said, *His Soul was grieved for their Miseries*, Judg. x. 16. If we consider the Life of our Blessed Saviour when on Earth, as it is recorded by his Followers, we shall find, that one uniform Desire for the eternal, and temporal Good of Mankind, discovered itself in all his Actions.

If we observe Men, both Apostles and others, in many different Ages, who have really come to the Unity of the Spirit, and the Fellowship of the Saints, there still appears the like Disposition, and in them the Desire of the real Happiness of Mankind, has out-ballanced the Desire of Ease, Liberty, and, many Times, Life itself.

If upon a true Search, we find that our Natures are so far renewed, that to exercise Righteousness and Loving Kindness [according to our Ability] towards all Men, without Respect of Persons, is easy to us, or is our Delight; if our Love be so orderly, and regular, that he who doth the Will of our Father, who is in Heaven, appears in our View, to be our nearest Relation, our Brother, and Sister, and Mother; if this be our Case, there is a good Foundation to hope, that the Blessing of God will sweeten our Treasures during our Stay in this Life, and our Memory be savory, when we are entered into Rest.

To conclude, 'Tis a Truth most certain, that a Life

guided by Wisdom from above, agreeable with Justice, Equity, and Mercy, is throughout consistent and amiable, and truly beneficial to Society; the Serenity and Calmness of Mind in it, affords an unparallel'd Comfort in this Life, and the End of it is blessed.

And, no less true, that they, who in the Midst of high Favours, remain ungrateful, and under all the Advantages that a Christian can desire, are selfish, earthly, and sensual, do miss the true Fountain of Happiness, and wander in a Maze of dark Anxiety, where all their Treasures are insufficient to quiet their Minds: Hence, from an insatiable Craving, they neglect doing Good with what they have acquired, and too often add Oppression to Vanity, that they may compass more.

O that they were wise, that they understood this, that they would consider their latter End! Deut. xxxii. 29.

THE END

CONSIDERATIONS
ON KEEPING NEGROES

Recommended to the Professors
of Christianity of every
Denomination
PART SECOND

By JOHN WOOLMAN

Ye shall not respect Persons in Judgement; but
you shall hear the Small as well as the Great:
You shall not be afraid of the Face of Man; for
the Judgement is God's. Deut. i. 17.

PHILADELPHIA
Printed by
B. Franklin & D. Hall 1762.

Newly printed at The Gehenna Press
Northampton 1970

THE PREFACE.

All our Actions are of like Nature with their Root; and the Most High weigheth them more skilfully than Men can weigh them one for another.

I believe that one Supreme Being made and supports the World; nor can I worship any other Deity without being an Idolater, and guilty of Wickedness.

Many Nations have believed in; and worshipped a Plurality of Deities; but I do not believe they were therefore all wicked.— Idolatry indeed is Wickedness; but it is the Thing, not the Name, which is so. Real Idolatry is to pay that Adoration to a Creature, which is known to be due only to the true GOD.

He who professeth to believe in one Almighty Creator, and in his Son JESUS CHRIST, *and is yet more intent on the Honours, Profits and Friendships of the World, than he is in Singleness of Heart to* stand faithful to the Christian Religion, *is in the Channel of Idolatry; while the* Gentile, *who, under some mistaken Opinions, is notwithstanding established in the true Principle of Virtue, and humbly adores an Almighty Power, may be of that Number who fear* GOD; *and work Righteousness.*

I believe the Bishop of Rome *assumes a Power, that does not belong to any Officer in the Church of* CHRIST; *and if I should knowingly do any Thing, tending to strengthen him in that Capacity, it would be great Iniquity. There are many Thousands of People, who by their Profession acknowledge him to be the Representative of* JESUS CHRIST *on Earth; and to say that none of them are upright in Heart, would be contrary to my Sentiments.*

Men who sincerely apply their Minds to true Virtue, and find an inward Support from above, by which all vicious Inclinations are made subject; that they love GOD sincerely, and prefer the real Good of Mankind universally to their own private Interest; though these, through the Strength of Education and Tradition, may remain under some speculative and great Errors, it would be uncharitable to say, that therefore GOD rejects them.—He who creates, supports and gives Understanding to all Men, his Knowledge and Goodness is superior to the various Cases and Circumstances of his Creatures, which to us appear the most difficult.

The Apostles and primitive Christians did not censure all the Gentiles as wicked Men, Rom. ii. 14. Col. iii. 2. but as they were favoured with a Gift to discern Things more clearly, respecting the Worship of the true GOD, they with much Firmness declared against the worshiping of Idols; and with true Patience endured many Sufferings, on that Account.

Great Numbers of faithful Protestants have contended for the Truth, in Opposition to Papal Errors; and with true Fortitude laid down their Lives in the Conflict, without saying, That no Man was saved who made Profession of that Religion.

While we have no Right to keep Men as Servants for Term of Life, but that of superior Power; to do this, with Design by their Labour to profit ourselves and our Families, I believe is wrong; but I do not believe that all who have kept Slaves, have therefore been chargeable with Guilt. If their Motives thereto were free from Selfishness, and their Slaves content, they were a Sort of Freemen; which I believe hath sometimes been the Case.

Whatever a Man does in the Spirit of Charity, to him it is not Sin: And while he lives and acts in this Spirit, he learns all Things essential to his Happiness, as an Individual: And if he doth not see that any Injury or Injustice, to any other Person, is necessarily promoted by any Part of his Form of Government, I believe the merciful Judge will not lay Iniquity to his Charge. Yet others, who live in the same Spirit of Charity, from a clear Convincement, may see the Relation of one Thing to another, and the necessary Tendency of each; and hence it may be absolutely binding on them to desist from some Parts of Conduct, which some good Men have been in.

CONSIDERATIONS
ON KEEPING
NEGROES, &c.

As some in most religious Societies amongst the *English* are concerned in importing or purchasing the Inhabitants of *Africa* as Slaves; and as the Professors of Christianity of several other Nations do the like; these Circumstances tend to make People less apt to examine the Practice so closely as they would, if such a Thing had not been, but was now proposed to be entered upon. It is however our Duty, and what concerns us individually, as Creatures accountable to our Creator, to employ rightly the Understanding which he hath given us, in humbly endeavouring to be acquainted with his Will concerning us, and with the Nature and Tendency of those Things which we practise: For as Justice remains to be Justice, so many People, of Reputation in the World, joining with wrong Things, do not excuse others in joining with them, nor make the Consequence of their Proceedings less dreadful in the final Issue, than it would be otherwise.

Where Unrighteousness is justified from one Age to another, it is like dark Matter gathering into Clouds over us. We may know that this Gloom will remain till the Cause be removed by a Reformation, or Change of Times; and may feel a Desire, from a

Love of Equity, to speak on the Occasion; yet where Error is so strong, that it may not be spoken against without some Prospect of Inconvenience to the Speaker, this Difficulty is likely to operate on our Weakness, and quench the good Desires in us; except we dwell so steadily under the Weight of it, as to be made willing to *endure Hardness* on that Account.

Where Men exert their Talents against Vices generally accounted such, the ill Effects whereof are presently perceived in a Government, all Men who regard their own temporal Good, are likely to approve the Work. But when that which is inconsistent with perfect Equity, hath the Law, or Countenance of the Great in its Favour, though the Tendency thereof be quite contrary to the true Happiness of Mankind in an equal, if not greater, Degree, than many Things accounted reproachful to Christians; yet as these ill Effects are not generally perceived, they who labour to dissuade from such Things, which People believe accord with their Interest, have many Difficulties to encounter.

The repeated Charges, which GOD gave to his Prophets, imply the Danger they were in of erring on this Hand. *Be not afraid of their Faces; for I am with thee, to deliver thee, saith the Lord,* Jer. i. 8. *Speak all the Words that I command thee to speak to them; diminish not a Word,* Jer. xxvi. 2. *And thou Son of Man, be not afraid of them,*

*nor dismayed at their Looks. Speak my Words to them,
whether they will hear or forbear,* Ezek. ii. 6.

Under an Apprehension of Duty, I offer some
further Considerations on this Subject, having
endeavoured some Years to consider it candidly.
I have observed People of our own Colour, whose
Abilities have been inferior to the Affairs which relate
to their convenient Subsistence, who have been
taken Care of by others, and the Profit of such Work
as they could do, applied toward their Support.–
I believe there are such amongst *Negroes*; and that
some People, in whose Hands they are, keep them
with no View of outward Profit, do not consider
them as black Men, who, as such, ought to serve
white Men; but account them Persons who have
Need of Guardians, and as such take Care of them:
Yet where equal Care is taken in all Parts of
Education, I do not apprehend Cases of this Sort
are likely to occur more frequently amongst one
Sort of People than another.

It looks to me that the Slave Trade was founded,
and hath generally been carried on, in a wrong Spirit;
that the Effects of it are detrimental to the real
Prosperity of our Country; and will be more so,
except we cease from the common Motives of
keeping them, and treat them in future agreeable to
Truth and pure Justice.

Negroes may be imported, who for their Cruelty to their Countrymen, and the evil Disposition of their Minds, may be unfit to be at Liberty; and if we, as Lovers of Righteousness, undertake the Management of them, we should have a full and clear Knowledge of their Crimes, and of those Circumstances which might operate in their Favour; but the Difficulty of obtaining this is so great, that we have great Reason to be cautious therein. But, should it plainly appear that absolute Subjection were a Condition the most proper for the Person who is purchased, yet the innocent Children ought not to be made Slaves, because their Parents sinned.

We have Account in Holy Scripture of some Families suffering, where mention is only made of the Heads of the Family committing Wickedness; and it is likely that the degenerate *Jews*, misunderstanding some Occurrences of this Kind, took Occasion to charge GOD with being unequal; so that a Saying became common, *The Fathers have eaten sour Grapes, and the Childrens Teeth are set on Edge.* *Jeremiah* and *Ezekiel*, two of the inspired Prophets, who lived near the same Time, were concerned to correct this Error. *Ezekiel* is large on the Subject. First, he reproves them for their Error. *What mean ye, that ye do so,* Chap. xviii. Verse 1. *As I live, saith the Lord God, ye shall not have Occasion any more to use this*

Proverb in Israel. The Words, *any more*, have Reference
to Time past; intimating, that though they had not
rightly understood some Things they had heard or
seen, and thence supposed the Proverb to be well
grounded; yet henceforth they might know of a
Certainty, that the Ways of GOD are all equal; that
as sure as the Most High liveth, so sure Men are
only answerable for their own Sins.—He thus sums
up the Matter; *The Soul that sinneth, it shall die. The Son
shall not bear the Iniquity of the Father; neither shall the Father
bear the Iniquity of the Son. The Righteousness of the Righteous
shall be upon him; and the Wickedness of the Wicked shall be
upon him.*

Where Men are wicked, they commonly are a
Means of corrupting the succeeding Age; and
thereby hasten those outward Calamities, which fall
on Nations, when their Iniquities are full.

Men may pursue Means which are not agreeable
to perfect Purity, with a View to increase the
Wealth and Happiness of their Offspring, and
thereby make the Way of Virtue more difficult to
them. And though the ill Example of a Parent, or a
Multitude, does not excuse a Man in doing Evil,
yet the Mind being early impressed with vicious
Notions and Practices, and nurtured up in Ways of
getting Treasure, which are not the Ways of Truth;
this wrong Spirit getting first Possession, and being

thus strengthened, frequently prevents due Attention to the true Spirit of Wisdom, so that they exceed in Wickedness those before them. And in this Channel, though Parents labour, as they think, to forward the Happiness of their Children, it proves a Means of forwarding their Calamity. This being the Case in the Age next before the grievous Calamity in the Siege of *Jerusalem*, and carrying *Judah* Captive to *Babylon*, they might say with Propriety, This came upon us, because our Fathers forsook GOD, and because we did worse than our Fathers.

As the Generation next before them inwardly turned away from GOD, who yet waited to be gracious; and as they in that Age continued in those Things which necessarily separated from perfect Goodness, growing more stubborn, till the Judgments of GOD were poured out upon them, they might properly say, *Our Fathers have sinned and we have borne their Iniquities*: And yet, wicked as their Fathers were, had they not succeeded them in their Wickedness, they had not borne their Iniquities.

To suppose it right, that an innocent Man shall at this Day be excluded from the common Rules of Justice; be deprived of that Liberty, which is the natural Right of human Creatures, and be a Slave to others during Life, on Account of a Sin committed by his immediate Parents; or a Sin committed by *Ham*, the Son of *Noah*; is a Supposition too gross to be admitted into the Mind of any Person, who sincerely desires to be governed by solid Principles.

It is alledged, in Favour of the Practice, that *Joshua* made Slaves of the *Gibeonites*.

What Men do by the Command of GOD, and what comes to pass as a Consequence of their Neglect, are different; such as the latter Case now mentioned was.

It was the express Command of the Almighty to *Israel*, concerning the Inhabitants of the promised Land, *Thou shalt make no Covenant with them, nor with their Gods: They shall not dwell in thy Land*, Exod. xxiii. 32. Those *Gibeonites* came craftily, telling *Joshua*, that they were come from a far Country; that their Elders had sent them to make a League with the People of *Israel*; and as an Evidence of their being Foreigners, shewed their old Cloaths, &c. *And the Men took of their Victuals, and asked not Counsel at the Mouth of the Lord; and* Joshua *made Peace with them, and made a League with them, to let them live; and the Princes sware to them.*

When the Imposition was discovered, the Congregation murmured against the Princes: *But all the Princes said to all the Congregation, we have sworn to them by the Lord God of Israel; now therefore we may not touch them; we will even let them live, lest Wrath be upon us;*

but let them be Hewers of Wood, and Drawers of Water
unto the Congregation.

Omitting to ask Counsel, involved them in great Difficulty. The *Gibeonites* were of those Cities, of which the LORD said, *Thou shalt save alive nothing that breatheth*; and of the Stock of the *Hivites,* concerning whom he commanded by Name, *Thou shalt smite them, and utterly destroy them: Thou shalt make no Covenant with them, nor shew Mercy unto them,* Deut. vii. 1. Thus *Joshua* and the Princes, not knowing them, had made a League with them, to let them live; and in this Strait they resolve to make them Servants. *Joshua* and the Princes suspected them to be Deceivers: *Peradventure you dwell amongst us; and how shall we make a League with you?* Which Words shew, that they remembered the Command before mentioned; and yet did not enquire at the Mouth of the LORD as *Moses* directed *Joshua*, when he gave him a Charge respecting his Duty as chief Man among the People, *Numb.* xxvii. 21. By this Omission Things became so situated, that *Joshua* and the Princes could not execute the Judgments of GOD on them, without violating the Oath which they had made.

Moses did amiss at the Waters of *Meribah*; and doubtless he soon repented; for the LORD was with him. And it is likely that *Joshua* was deeply humbled, under a Sense of his Omission; for it appears that GOD continued him in his Office, and spared the Lives of those People, for the Sake of the League and Oath made in his Name.

The Wickedness of these People was great, and they worthy to die, or perfect Justice had not passed Sentence of Death upon them; and as their Execution was prevented by this League and Oath, they appear content to be Servants: *As it seemeth good and right unto thee to do unto us, do.*

These Criminals, instead of Death, had the Sentence of Servitude pronounced on them, in these Words, *Now therefore ye are cursed; and there shall none of you be freed from being Bondmen, and Hewers of Wood, and Drawers of Water for the House of my God.*

We find, *Deut.* xx. 10. that there were Cities far distant from *Canaan*, against which *Israel* went to Battle; unto whom they were to proclaim Peace, and if the Inhabitants made Answer of Peace, and opened their Gates, they were not to destroy them, but make them Tributaries.

The Children of *Israel* were then the LORD'S Host, and Executioners of his Judgments on People hardened in Wickedness.—They were not to go to Battle, but by his Appointment. The Men who were chief in his Army, had their Instructions from the Almighty; sometimes immediately, and sometimes by the Ministry of Angels. Of these, amongst others, were *Moses, Joshua, Othniel,* and *Gideon;* See *Exod.* iii. 2. and xviii. 19. *Josh.* v. 13. These People far off from *Canaan,* against whom *Israel* was sent to Battle, were so corrupt, that the Creator of the Universe saw it good to change their Situation; and in case of their opening their Gates, and coming under Tribute, this their Subjection, though probably more mild than absolute Slavery, was to last little or no longer than while *Israel* remained in the true Spirit of Government.

It was pronounced by *Moses* the Prophet, as a Consequence of their Wickedness, *The Stranger that is within thee shall get above thee very high; and thou shalt come down very low: He shall be the Head, and thou the Tail.*

This we find in some Measure verified in their being made Tributaries to the *Moabites, Midianites, Amorites* and *Philistines.*

It is alledged in Favour of the Practice of Slave-keeping, that the *Jews* by their Law made Slaves of the Heathen, *Levit.* xxv. 45. *Moreover, of the Children of the Stranger that do sojourn amongst you, of them shall ye buy, and of their Children, which are with you, which they beget in your Land; and they shall be your Possession; and you shall take them as an Inheritance for your Children after you, to inherit them as a Possession, they shall be your Bondmen for ever.*—It is difficult for us to have any certain Knowledge of the Mind of *Moses*, in Regard to keeping Slaves, any other Way than by looking upon him as a true Servant of GOD, whose Mind and Conduct were regulated by an inward Principle of Justice and Equity. To admit a Supposition that he in that Case was drawn from perfect Equity by the Alliance of outward Kindred, would be to disown his Authority.

Abraham had Servants born in his House, and bought with his Money: *And the Almighty said of Abraham, I know him, that he will order his House after him.* Which implies, that he was as a Father, an Instructor, and a good Governor over his People.—And *Moses*, considered as a Man of GOD must necessarily have had a Prospect of some real Advantage in the Strangers and Heathens being Servants to the *Israelites* for a Time.

As Mankind had received and established many erroneous Opinions and hurtful Customs, their living and conversing with the *Jews*, while the *Jews* stood faithful to their Principles, might be helpful to remove those Errors, and reform their Manners.— But for Men, with private Views, to assume an absolute Power over the Persons and Properties of others; and continue it from Age to Age in the Line of natural Generation, without Regard to the Virtues and Vices of their Successors, as it is manifestly contrary to true universal Love, and attended with great Evils, there requires the clearest Evidence to beget a Belief in us, that *Moses* intended that the Strangers should as such be Slaves to the *Jews*.

He directed them to buy Strangers and Sojourners.— It appears that there were Strangers in *Israel* who were free Men; and considering with what Tenderness and Humanity the *Jews*, by their Law, were obliged to use their Servants, and what Care was to be taken to instruct them in the true Religion, it is not unlikely that some Strangers in Poverty and Distress were willing to enter into Bonds to serve the *Jews* as long as they lived; and in such Case the *Jews*, by their Law, had a Right to their Service during Life.

When the Awl was bored through the Ear of the *Hebrew* Servant, the Text saith, *He shall serve for ever*; yet we do not suppose that by the Word *for ever*, it was intended that none of his Posterity should afterwards be free; when it is said in Regard to the Strangers which they bought, *They shall be your Possession*, it may be well understood to mean only the Persons so purchased; all preceding relates to buying them; and what follows, to the Continuance of their Service. *You shall take them as an Inheritance to your Children after you; they shall be your Bondmen for ever.* It may be well understood to stand limited to those they purchased.

Moses, directing *Aaron* and his Sons to wash their Hands and Feet, when they went into the Tabernacle of the Congregation, saith, *It shall be a Statute for ever to them, even to him and his Seed throughout all Generations.* And to express the Continuance of the Law, it was his common Language, *It shall be a Statute for ever throughout your Generations.* So that had he intended the Posterity of the Strangers so purchased to continue in Slavery to the *Jews*, it looks likely that he would have used some Terms clearly to express it. The *Jews* undoubtedly had Slaves, whom they kept as such from one Age to another; but that this was agreeable to the genuine Design of their inspired Law-giver, is far from being a clear Case.

Making Constructions of the Law contrary to the true Meaning of it, was common amongst that People.—*Samuel's* Sons took Bribes, and perverted Judgment.—*Isaiah* complained that they justified the Wicked for Reward.—*Zephaniah*, Cotemporary with *Jeremiah*, on Account of the Injustice of the civil Magistrates, declared that those Judges were Evening Wolves; and that the Priests did Violence to the Law.

Jeremiah acquaints us, that the Priests cried Peace, Peace, when there was no Peace; by which Means the People grew bold in their Wickedness; and having committed Abominations, were not ashamed; but, through wrong Constructions of the Law, they justified themselves, and boastingly said, *We are wise;*

46

and the Law of the Lord is with us. These Corruptions continued till the Days of our Saviour, who told the *Pharisees, You have made the Commandment of God of none Effect through your Tradition.*

Thus it appears that they corrupted the Law of *Moses*; nor is it unlikely that among many others this was one; for oppressing the Strangers was a heavy Charge against the *Jews*, and very often strongly represented by the Lord's faithful Prophets.

That the Liberty of Man was, by the inspired Law-giver, esteemed precious, appears in this; that such who unjustly deprived Men of it, were to be punished in like Manner as if they had murdered them. *He that stealeth a Man, and selleth him; or if he be found in his Hand, shall surely be put to Death.* This Part of the Law was so considerable, that *Paul*, the learned *Jew*, giving a brief Account of the Uses of the Law, adds this, *It was made for Men-stealers*, 1 Tim. i. 10.

The great Men amongst that People were exceeding oppressive; and, it is likely, exerted their whole Strength and Influence to have the Law construed to suit their Turns.—The honest Servants of the Lord had heavy Work with them in regard to their Oppression; a few Instances follow. *Thus saith the Lord of Hosts, the God of Israel, amend your Ways, and your Doings; and I will cause you to dwell in this Place. If you thoroughly execute Judgment between a Man and his Neighbour;*

47

if you oppress not the Stranger, the Fatherless and the Widow; and shed not innocent Blood in this Place; neither walk after other Gods to your Hurt, then will I cause you to dwell in this Place, Jer. vii.—Again a Message was sent not only to the inferior Ministers of Justice, but also to the chief Ruler. *Thus saith the Lord, go down to the House of the King of* Judah, *and speak there this Word; execute ye Judgment and Righteousness, and deliver the Spoiled out of the Hand of the Oppressor; and do no Wrong; do no Violence to the Stranger, the Fatherless and the Widow; neither shed innocent Blood in this Place.* Then adds, *That in so doing they should prosper; but if ye will not hear these Words, I swear by myself, saith the Lord, that this House shall become a Desolation,* Jer. xxii.

The King, the Princes and Rulers were agreed in Oppression before the *Babylonish* Captivity; for whatever Courts of Justice were retained amongst them; or however they decided Matters betwixt Men of Estates, it is plain that the Cause of the Poor was not judged in Equity.

It appears that the great Men amongst the *Jews* were fully resolved to have Slaves, even of their own Brethren, *Jer.* xxxiv. Notwithstanding the Promises and Threatenings of the LORD, by the Prophet, and their solemn Covenant to set them free, confirmed by the Imprecation of passing between the Parts of a Calf cut in twain; intimating, by that Ceremony, that on Breach of the Covenant, it were just for their Bodies to be so cut in Pieces.—Yet after all, they held fast to their old Custom, and called Home the Servants whom they had set free.—*And ye were now turned, and had done right in my Sight, in proclaiming Liberty every Man to his Neighbour; and ye had made a Covenant before me, in the House which is called by my Name; but ye turned, and polluted my Name; and caused every Man his Servant, whom he had set at Liberty at their Pleasure, to return, and brought them into Subjection, to be unto you for Servants, and for Handmaids: Therefore thus saith the Lord, ye have not hearkened unto me, in proclaiming Liberty every one to his Neighbour, and every one to his Brother. Behold, I proclaim Liberty to you, saith the Lord, to the Sword, to the Pestilence, and to the Famine; and I will make you to be removed into all the Kingdoms of the Earth.—The Men who transgressed my Covenant which they made, and passed .between the Parts of the Calf, I will give into the Hands of their Enemies, and their dead Bodies shall be for Meat unto the Fowls of the Heaven, and the Beasts of the Earth.*

Soon after this their City was taken and burnt; the King's Sons and the Princes slain; and the King, with the chief Men of his Kingdom, carried Captive to *Babylon.—Ezekiel*, prophesying the Return of that People to their own Land, directs, *Ye shall divide the Land by Lot, for an Inheritance unto you, and to the Strangers that sojourn amongst you; in what Tribe the Stranger sojourns,*

there shall ye give him his Inheritance, saith the Lord God.
Nor is this particular Direction, and the Authority
with which it is enforced, without a tacit Implication,
that their Ancestors had erred in their Conduct
towards the Stranger.

Some who keep Slaves, have doubted as to the
Equity of the Practice; but as they knew Men, noted
for their Piety, who were in it, this, they say, has
made their Minds easy.

To lean on the Example of Men in doubtful Cases,
is difficult: For only admit, that those Men were not
faithful and upright to the highest Degree, but that
in some particular Case they erred, and it may follow
that this one Case was the same, about which we are
in Doubt; and to quiet our Minds by their Example,
may be dangerous to ourselves; and continuing in it,
prove a Stumbling-block to tender-minded People
who succeed us, in like Manner as their Examples
are to us.

But supposing Charity was their only Motive, and
they not foreseeing the Tendency of paying Robbers
for their Booty, were not justly under the Imputation
of being Partners with a Thief, *Prov.* xxix. 24. but
were really innocent in what they did, are we assured
that we keep them with the same Views they kept
them? If we keep them from no other Motive than a
real Sense of Duty, and true Charity governs us in

all our Proceedings toward them, we are so far safe: But if another Spirit, which inclines our Minds to the Ways of this World, prevail upon us, and we are concerned for our own outward Gain more than for their real Happiness, it will avail us nothing that some good Men have had the Care and Management of *Negroes*.

Since Mankind spread upon the Earth, many have been the Revolutions attending the several Families, and their Customs and Ways of Life different from each other. This Diversity of Manners, though some are preferable to others, operates not in Favour of any, so far as to justify them to do Violence to innocent Men; to bring them from their own to another Way of Life. The Mind, when moved by a Principle of true Love, may feel a Warmth of Gratitude to the universal Father, and a lively Sympathy with those Nations, where Divine Light has been less manifest.

This Desire for their real Good may beget a Willingness to undergo Hardships for their Sakes, that the true Knowledge of GOD may be spread amongst them: But to take them from their own Land, with Views of Profit to ourselves, by Means inconsistent with pure Justice, is foreign to that Principle which seeks the Happiness of the whole Creation. Forced Subjection, on innocent Persons of full Age, is inconsistent with right Reason; on one Side, the human Mind is not naturally fortified with that Firmness in Wisdom and Goodness, necessary to an independent Ruler; on the other Side, to be subject to the uncontroulable Will of a Man, liable to err, is most painful and afflicting to a conscientious Creature.

It is our Happiness faithfully to serve the Divine Being, who made us: His Perfection makes our Service reasonable; but so long as Men are biassed by narrow Self-love, so long an absolute Power over other Men is unfit for them.

Men, taking on them the Government of others, may intend to govern reasonably, and make their Subjects more happy than they would be otherwise; but, as absolute Command belongs only to him who is perfect, where frail Men, in their own Wills, assume such Command, it hath a direct Tendency to vitiate their Minds, and make them more unfit for Government.

Placing on Men the ignominious Title SLAVE, dressing them in uncomely Garments, keeping them to servile Labour, in which they are often dirty, tends gradually to fix a Notion in the Mind, that they are a Sort of People below us in Nature, and leads us to consider them as such in all our Conclusions about them. And, moreover, a Person

which in our Esteem is mean and contemptible, if
their Language or Behaviour toward us is unseemly
or disrespectful, it excites Wrath more powerfully
than the like Conduct in one we accounted our
Equal or Superior; and where this happens to be the
Case, it disqualifies for candid Judgment; for it is
unfit for a Person to sit as Judge in a Case where his
own personal Resentments are stirred up; and, as
Members of Society in a well framed Government,
we are mutually dependant. Present Interest incites
to Duty, and makes each Man attentive to the
Convenience of others; but he whose Will is a Law
to others, and can enforce Obedience by Punishment;
he whose Wants are supplied without feeling any
Obligation to make equal Returns to his Benefactor,
his irregular Appetites find an open Field for
Motion, and he is in Danger of growing hard, and
inattentive to their Convenience who labour for his
Support; and so loses that Disposition, in which
alone Men are fit to govern.

The *English* Government hath been commended
by candid Foreigners for the Disuse of Racks and
Tortures, so much practised in some States; but this
multiplying Slaves now leads to it; for where People
exact hard Labour of others, without a suitable
Reward, and are resolved to continue in that Way,
Severity to such who oppose them becomes the

Consequence; and several *Negroe* Criminals, among the *English* in *America*, have been executed in a lingering, painful Way, very terrifying to others.

It is a happy Case to set out right, and persevere in the same Way: A wrong Beginning leads into many Difficulties; for to support one Evil, another becomes customary; two produces more; and the further Men proceed in this Way, the greater their Dangers, their Doubts and Fears; and the more painful and perplexing are their Circumstances; so that such who are true Friends to the real and lasting Interest of our Country, and candidly consider the Tendency of Things, cannot but feel some Concern on this Account.

There is that Superiority in Men over the Brute Creatures, and some of them so manifestly dependant on Men for a Living, that for them to serve us in Moderation, so far as relates to the right Use of Things, looks consonant to the Design of our Creator.

There is nothing in their Frame, nothing relative to the propagating their Species, which argues the contrary; but in Men there is. The Frame of Mens Bodies, and the Disposition of their Minds are different; some, who are tough and strong, and their Minds active, chuse Ways of Life requiring much Labour to support them; others are soon weary; and though Use makes Labour more tolerable, yet some are less apt for Toil than others, and their Minds less sprightly. These latter labouring for their Subsistance, commonly chuse a Life easy to support, being content with a little. When they are weary they may rest, take the most advantageous Part of the Day for Labour; and in all Cases proportion one Thing to another, that their Bodies be not oppressed.

Now, while each is at Liberty, the latter may be as happy, and live as comfortably as the former; but where Men of the first Sort have the latter under absolute Command, not considering the Odds in Strength and Firmness, do, sometimes, in their eager Pursuit, lay on Burthens grievous to be borne; by Degrees grow rigorous, and, aspiring to Greatness, they increase Oppression, and the true Order of kind Providence is subverted.

There are Weaknesses sometimes attending us, which make little or no Alteration in our Countenances, nor much lessen our Appetite for Food, and yet so affect us, as to make Labour very uneasy. In such Case Masters, intent on putting forward Business, and jealous of the Sincerity of their Slaves, may disbelieve what they say, and grievously afflict them.

Action is necessary for all Men, and our exhausting Frame requires a Support, which is the Fruit of

Action. The Earth must be laboured to keep us alive: Labour is a proper Part of our Life; to make one answer the other in some useful Motion, looks agreeable to the Design of our Creator. Motion, rightly managed, tends to our Satisfaction, Health and Support.

Those who quit all useful Business, and live wholly on the Labour of others, have their Exercise to seek; some such use less than their Health requires; others chuse that which, by the Circumstances attending it, proves utterly reverse to true Happiness. Thus, while some are diverse Ways distressed for Want of an open Channel of useful Action, those who support them sigh, and are exhausted in a Stream too powerful for Nature, spending their Days with too little Cessation from Labour.

Seed sown with the Tears of a confined oppressed People, Harvest cut down by an overborne discontented Reaper, makes Bread less sweet to the Taste of an honest Man, than that which is the Produce, or just Reward of such voluntary Action, which is one proper Part of the Business of human Creatures.

Again, the weak State of the human Species, in bearing and bringing forth their Young, and the helpless Condition of their Young beyond that of other Creatures, clearly shew that *Perfect Goodness* designs a tender Care and Regard should be exercised toward them; and that no imperfect, arbitrary Power should prevent the cordial Effects of that Sympathy, which is, in the Minds of well-met Pairs, to each other, and toward their Offspring.

In our Species the mutual Ties of Affection are more rational and durable than in others below us; the Care and Labour of raising our Offspring much greater. The Satisfaction arising to us in their innocent Company, and in their Advances from one rational Improvement to another, is considerable, when two are thus joined, and their Affections sincere; it however happens among Slaves, that they are often situate in different Places; and their seeing each other depends on the Will of Men, liable to human Passions, and a Byas in Judgment; who, with Views of Self-interest, may keep them apart more than is right. Being absent from each other, and often with other Company, there is a Danger of their Affections being alienated, Jealousies arising, the Happiness otherwise resulting from their Offspring frustrated, and the Comforts of Marriage destroyed.— These Things being considered closely, as happening to a near Friend, will appear to be hard and painful.

He who reverently observes that Goodness manifested by our Gracious Creator toward the various Species of Beings in this World, will see, that in our Frame and Constitution is clearly shewn that innocent Men, capable to manage for themselves, were not intended to be Slaves.

A person lately travelling amongst the *Negroes* near *Senegal*, hath this Remark; "Which Way soever I "turned my Eyes on this pleasant Spot, I beheld a "perfect Image of pure Nature; an agreeable "Solitude, bounded on every Side by charming "Landskips, the rural Situation of Cottages in the "Midst of Trees. The Ease and Indolence of the "*Negroes* reclined under the Shade of their spreading "Foliage; the Simplicity of their Dress and Manners; "the Whole revived in my Mind the Idea of our "first Parents, and I seemed to contemplate the "World in its primitive State." *M. Adanson*, Page 55.

Some *Negroes* in these Parts, who have had an agreeable Education, have manifested a Brightness of Understanding equal to many of us. A Remark of this Kind we find in *Bosman*, Page 328. "The *Negroes* "of *Fida*, saith he, are so accurately quick in their "Merchandize Accounts, that they easily reckon as "justly and quickly in their Heads only, as we with "the Assistance of Pen and Ink, though the Sum "amounts to several Thousands."

Through the Force of long Custom, it appears needful to speak in Relation to Colour.—Suppose a

58

white Child, born of Parents of the meanest Sort, who died and left him an Infant, falls into the Hands of a Person, who endeavours to keep him a Slave, some Men would account him an unjust Man in doing so, who yet appear easy while many Black People, of honest Lives, and good Abilities, are enslaved, in a Manner more shocking than the Case here supposed. This is owing chiefly to the Idea of Slavery being connected with the Black Colour, and Liberty with the White:—And where false Ideas are twisted into our Minds, it is with Difficulty we get fairly disentangled.

A Traveller, in cloudy Weather, misseth his Way, makes many Turns while he is lost; still forms in his Mind the Bearing and Situation of Places, and though the Ideas are wrong, they fix as fast as if they were right. Finding how Things are, we see our Mistake; yet the Force of Reason, with repeated Observations on Places and Things, do not soon remove those false Notions, so fastened upon us, but it will seem in the Imagination as if the annual Course of the Sun was altered; and though, by Recollection, we are assured it is not, yet those Ideas do not suddenly leave us.

Selfishness being indulged, clouds the Understanding; and where selfish Men, for a long Time, proceed on their Way, without Opposition, the Deceiveableness of Unrighteousness gets so rooted in their Intellects, that a candid Examination of Things relating to Self-interest is prevented; and in this Circumstance, some who would not agree to make a Slave of a Person whose Colour is like their own, appear easy in making Slaves of others of a different Colour, though their Understandings and Morals are equal to the Generality of Men of their own Colour.

The Colour of a Man avails nothing, in Matters of Right and Equity. Consider Colour in Relation to Treaties; by such, Disputes betwixt Nations are sometimes settled. And should the Father of us all so dispose Things, that Treaties with black Men should sometimes be necessary, how then would it appear amongst the Princes and Ambassadors, to insist on the Prerogative of the white Colour?

Whence is it that Men, who believe in a righteous Omnipotent Being, to whom all Nations stand equally related, and are equally accountable, remain so easy in it; but for that the Ideas of *Negroes* and Slaves are so interwoven in the Mind, that they do not discuss this Matter with that Candour and Freedom of Thought, which the Case justly calls for?

To come at a right Feeling of their Condition, requires humble serious Thinking; for, in their present Situation, they have but little to engage our natural Affection in their Favour.

Had we a Son or a Daughter involved in the same Case, in which many of them are, it would alarm us, and make us feel their Condition without seeking for it. The Adversity of an intimate Friend will incite our Compassion, while others, equally good, in the like Trouble, will but little affect us.

Again, the Man in worldly Honour, whom we consider as our Superior, treating us with Kindness and Generosity, begets a Return of Gratitude and Friendship toward him. We may receive as great Benefits from Men a Degree lower than ourselves, in the common Way of reckoning, and feel ourselves less engaged in Favour of them. Such is our Condition by Nature; and these Things being narrowly watched and examined, will be found to center in Self-love.

The Blacks seem far from being our Kinsfolks, and did we find an agreeable Disposition and sound Understanding in some of them, which appeared as a good Foundation for a true Friendship between us, the Disgrace arising from an open Friendship with a Person of so vile a Stock, in the common Esteem, would naturally tend to hinder it.—They have neither Honours, Riches, outward Magnificence nor Power; their Dress coarse, and often ragged; their

Employ Drudgery, and much in the Dirt: They have little or nothing at Command; but must wait upon and work for others, to obtain the Necessaries of Life; so that, in their present Situation, there is not much to engage the Friendship, or move the Affection of selfish Men: But such who live in the Spirit of true Charity, to sympathise with the Afflicted in the lowest Stations of Life, is a Thing familiar to them.

Such is the Kindness of our Creator, that People, applying their Minds to sound Wisdom, may, in general, with moderate Exercise, live comfortably, where no misapplied Power hinders it.—We in these Parts have Cause gratefully to acknowledge it. But Men leaving the true Use of Things, their Lives are less calm, and have less of real Happiness in them.

Many are desirous of purchasing and keeping Slaves, that they may live in some Measure conformable to those Customs of the Times, which have in them a Tincture of Luxury; for when we, in the least Degree, depart from that Use of the Creatures, which the Creator of all Things intended for them, there Luxury begins.

And if we consider this Way of Life seriously, we shall see there is nothing in it sufficient to induce a wise Man to chuse it, before a plain, simple Way of living. If we examine stately Buildings and

Equipage, delicious Food, superfine Cloaths, Silks
and Linens; if we consider the Splendour of choice
Metal fastened upon Raiment, and the most showy
Inventions of Men, it will yet appear that the
humble-minded Man, who is contented with the
true Use of Houses, Food and Garments, and
chearfully exerciseth himself agreeable to his Station
in Civil Society, to earn them, acts more reasonably,
and discovers more Soundness of Understanding in
his Conduct, than such who lay heavy Burdens on
others, to support themselves in a luxurious Way of
living.

   George Buchanan, in his History of *Scotland*, Page 62,
tells of some ancient Inhabitants of *Britain*, who were
derived from a People that "had a Way of marking
"their Bodies, as some said, with Instruments of
"Iron, with Variety of Pictures, and with Animals
"of all Shapes, and wear no Garments, that they
"should not hide their Pictures; and were therefore
"called *Picts*."

   Did we see those People shrink with Pain, for a
considerable Time together, under the Point or
Edge of this Iron Instrument, and their Bodies all
bloody with the Operation; did we see them
sometimes naked, suffering with Cold, and refuse to
put on Garments, that those imaginary Ensigns of
Grandeur might not be concealed, it is likely we

should pity their Folly, and Fondness for those Things: But if we candidly compare their Conduct, in that Case, with some Conduct amongst ourselves, will it not appear that our Folly is the greatest?

In true Gospel Simplicity, free from all wrong Use of Things, a Spirit which breathes Peace and good Will is cherished; but when we aspire after imaginary Grandeur, and apply to selfish Means to attain our End, this Desire, in its Original, is the same with the *Picts* in cutting Figures on their Bodies; but the evil Consequences attending our Proceedings are the greatest.

A covetous Mind, which seeks Opportunity to exalt itself, is a great Enemy to true Harmony in a Country: Envy and Grudging usually accompany this Disposition, and it tends to stir up its Likeness in others. And where this Disposition ariseth so high, as to embolden us to look upon honest industrious Men as our own Property during Life, and to keep them to hard Labour, to support us in those Customs which have not their Foundation in right Reason; or to use any Means of Oppression, a haughty Spirit is cherished on one Side, and the Desire of Revenge frequently on the other, till the Inhabitants of the Land are ripe for great Commotion and Trouble; and thus Luxury and Oppression have the Seeds of War and Desolation in them.

Some Account of the Slave-Trade,
From the Writings of Persons who have been at the
Places where they are first purchased, viz.

Bosman on *Guiney*, who was a Factor for the *Dutch*
about sixteen Years in that Country [Page 339] thus
remarks: "But since I have so often mentioned that
"Commerce, I shall describe how it is managed by
"our Factors. The first Business of one of our
"Factors, when he comes to *Fida*, is to satisfy the
"Customs of the King, and the great Men, which
"amounts to about *One Hundred Pounds*, in *Guiney*
"Value, as the Goods must sell there. After which we
"have free Licence to trade, which is published
"throughout the whole Land by the Cryer. And yet
"before we can deal with any Person, we are obliged
"to buy the King's whole Stock of Slaves, at a set
"Price; which is commonly one Third or Fourth
"higher than ordinary. After which, we have free
"Leave to deal with all his Subjects, of what Rank
"soever. But if there happen to be no Stock of Slaves,
"the Factor must resolve to run the Risk of trusting
"the Inhabitants with Goods, to the Value of One or
"Two Hundred Slaves; which Commodities they
"send into the Inland Country, in order to buy with
"them Slaves at all Markets, and that sometimes
"Two Hundred Miles deep in the Country: For you
"ought to be informed, that Markets of Men are

"here kept in the same Manner as they of Beasts are
"with us.

    "Most of the Slaves which are offered to us, are
"Prisoners of War, which are sold by the Victors as
"their Booty.—When these Slaves come to *Fida*, they
"are put in Prisons all together; and when we treat
"concerning them, they are all brought out in a large
"Plain, where, by our Surgeons, whose Province it is,
"they are thoroughly examined, even to the smallest
"Member, and that naked, both Men and Women,
"without the least Distinction or Modesty. Those
"which are approved as good, are set on one Side.
"The Invalids and Maimed being thrown out, the
"Remainder are numbered, and it is entered who
"delivered them: In the mean while a burning Iron,
"with the Arms or Name of the Company, lies in
"the Fire, with which ours are marked on the Breast.
"This is done, that we may distinguish them from
"the Slaves of the *English*, *French*, or others. When we
"have agreed with the Owners of the Slaves, they are
"returned to their Prisons, where, from that Time
"forward, they are kept at our Charge, cost us
"*Two-pence* a Day a Slave, which serves to subsist
"them, like our Criminals, on Bread and Water:
"So that, to save Charges, we send them on board
"our Ships the first Opportunity; before which their
"Masters strip them of all they have on their Backs,

"so that they come aboard stark naked, as well
"Women as Men; in which Condition they are
"obliged to continue, if the Master of the Ship is not
"so charitable [which he commonly is] as to bestow
"something on them, to cover their Nakedness.

"The Inhabitants of *Popo*, as well as those of *Coto*,
"depend on Plunder, and the Slave-Trade, in both
"which they very much exceed the latter; for being
"endowed with more Courage, they rob more
"successfully, and by that Means increase their
"Trade: Notwithstanding which, to freight a Vessel
"with Slaves, requires some Months Attendance.
"In the Year 1697, in three Days Time I could get
"but three Slaves; but they assured me, that if I
"would have Patience for other three Days only,
"they should be able to deliver me One or Two
"Hundred." Same Author, Page 310.

"We cast Anchor at *Cape Mizurada*, but not one
"*Negroe* coming on board, I went on Shore; and being
"desirous to be informed why they did not come on
"board, was answered, That about two Months
"before the *English* had been there, with two Vessels,
"and had ravaged the Country, destroyed all their
"Canoes, plundered their Houses, and carried off
"some of their People for Slaves; upon which the
"Remainder fled to the Inland Country. They tell us,
"they live in Peace with all their Neighbours, and

67

"have no Notion of any other Enemy than the
"*English*; of which Nation they had taken some then:
"And publickly declared, that they would endeavour
"to get as many of them, as the two mentioned Ships
"had carried off of their Natives. These unhappy
"*English* were in Danger of being sacrificed to the
"Memory of their Friends, which some of their
"Nation carried off." *Bosman*, Page 440.

Extracts from a Collection of
Voyages. Vol. I.

The Author, a *Popish* Missionary, speaking of his
departing from the *Negroe* Country to *Brazil*, saith,
"I remember the Duke of *Bambay* [a *Negroe* Chief]
"one Day sent me several Blacks, to be my Slaves,
"which I would not accept of; but sent them back to
"him. I afterwards told him, I came not into his
"Country to make Slaves; but rather to deliver those
"from the Slavery of the Devil, whom he kept in
"miserable Thraldom. The Ship I went aboard was
"loaded with Elephants Teeth, and Slaves, to the
"Number of Six Hundred and Eighty Men,
"Women and Children. It was a pitiful Sight to
"behold how all these People were bestowed. The
"Men were standing in the Hold, fastened one to
"another with Stakes, for Fear they should rise, and
"kill the Whites: The Women were between the
"Decks, and those that were with Child in the Great

"Cabbin: The Children in the Steerage, pressed
"together like Herrings in a Barrel; which caused an
"intolerable Heat and Stench." Page 507.

"It is now Time [saith the same Author] to speak
"of a brutish Custom these People have amongst
"them, in making Slaves; which I take not to be
"lawful for any Person of a good Conscience to buy."—

He then describes how Women betray Men into
Slavery, and adds, "There are others going up into
"the Inland Country, and, through Pretence of
"Jurisdiction, seize Men upon any trifling Offence,
"and sell them for Slaves." Page 537.

The Author of this Treatise, conversing with a
Person of good Credit, was informed by him, that
in his Youth, while in *England*, he was minded to
come to *America*, and happening on a Vessel bound for
Guiney, and from thence into *America*, he, with a
View to see *Africa*, went on board her, and continued
with them in their Voyage, and so came into this
Country. Among other Circumstances he related
these. "They purchased on the Coast about Three
"Hundred Slaves; some of them he understood were
"Captives of War; some stolen by other *Negroes*
"privately.—When they had got many Slaves on
"board, but were still on that Coast, a Plot was laid by
"an old *Negroe*, notwithstanding the Men had Irons
"on their Hands and Feet, to kill the *English*, and

"take the Vessel; which being discovered, the Man
"was hanged, and many of the Slaves made to shoot
"at him as he hung up.

"Another Slave was charged with having a Design
"to kill the *English*; and the Captain spoke to him in
"Relation to the Charge brought against him, as he
"stood on Deck; whereupon he immediately threw
"himself into the Sea, and was drowned.

"Several *Negroes*, confined on board, were, he said,
"so extremely uneasy with their Condition, that
"after many Endeavours used, they could never make
"them eat nor drink after they came in the Vessel;
"but in a desperate Resolution starved themselves to
"Death, behaving toward the last like Mad-men."

In *Randall's* Geography, printed 1744, we are
informed, "That in a Time of full Peace nothing is
"more common than for the *Negroes* of one Nation to
"steal those of another, and sell them to the *Europeans*.
"It is thought that the *English* transmit annually near
"Fifty Thousand of these unhappy Creatures; and
"the other *European* Nations together, about Two
"Hundred Thousand more."

It is through the Goodness of GOD that the
Reformation from gross Idolatry and Barbarity hath
been thus far effected; if we consider our Conditions
as Christians, and the Benefits we enjoy, and
compare them with the Condition of those People,

and consider that our Nation trading with them for their Country Produce, have had an Opportunity of imparting useful Instructions to them, and remember that but little Pains have been taken therein, it must look like an Indifference in us.—But when we reflect on a Custom the most shocking of any amongst them, and remember that, with a View to outward Gain, we have joined as Parties in it; that our Concurrence with them in their barbarous Proceedings, has tended to harden them in Cruelty, and been a Means of increasing Calamities in their Country, we must own that herein we have acted contrary to those Worthies whose Lives and Substance were spent in propagating Truth and Righteousness amongst the Heathen. When *Saul*, by the Hand of *Doeg*, slew Four Score Priests at once, he had a Jealousy that one of them at least was confederate with *David*, whom he considered as his Enemy.— *Herod* slaying all the Male Children in *Bethlehem* of two Years old and under, was an Act of uncommon Cruelty; but he supposed there was a Male Child there, within that Age, who was likely to be King of the *Jews*, and finding no Way to destroy him, but by destroying them all, thought this the most effectual Means to secure the Kingdom to his own Family.

When the Sentence against the Protestants of

Marindol, &c. in *France*, was put in Execution, great Numbers of People fled to the Wilderness; amongst whom were ancient People, Women great with Child, and others with Babes in their Arms, who endured Calamities grievous to relate, and in the End some perished with Hunger, and many were destroyed by Fire and Sword; but they had this Objection against them, That they obstinately persisted in Opposition to Holy Mother Church, and being Hereticks, it was right to work their Ruin and Extirpation, and raze out their Memory from among Men. Foxe's *Acts and Monuments*, Page 646.

In Favour of those Cruelties, every one had what they deemed a Plea.—These Scenes of Blood and Cruelty among the barbarous Inhabitants of *Guiney*, are not less terrible than those now mentioned. They are continued from one Age to another, and we make ourselves Parties and Fellow-helpers in them; nor do I see that we have any Plea in our Favour more plausible than the Plea of *Saul*, of *Herod*, or the *French* in those Slaughters.

Many who are Parties in this Trade, by keeping Slaves with Views of Self-interest, were they to go as Soldiers in one of these Inland Expeditions to catch Slaves, they must necessarily grow dissatisfied with such Employ, or cease to profess their religious Principles. And though the first and most striking

Part of the Scene is done at a great Distance, and by other Hands, yet every one who is acquainted with the Circumstances, and notwithstanding joins in it for the Sake of Gain only, must, in the Nature of Things, be chargeable with the others.

Should we consider ourselves present as Spectators, when cruel *Negroes* privately catch innocent Children, who are employed in the Fields; hear their lamentable Cries, under the most terrifying Apprehensions; or should we look upon it as happening in our own Families, having our Children carried off by Savages, we must needs own, that such Proceedings are contrary to the Nature of Christianity: Should we meditate on the Wars which are greatly increased by this Trade, and on that Affliction which many Thousands live in, through Apprehensions of being taken or slain; on the Terror and Amazement that Villages are in, when surrounded by these Troops of Enterprisers; on the great Pain and Misery of groaning dying Men, who get wounded in those Skirmishes; we shall necessarily see, that it is impossible to be Parties in such a Trade, on the Motives of Gain, and retain our Innocence.

Should we consider the Case of Multitudes of those People, who in a fruitful Soil, and hot Climate, with a little Labour, raise Grain, Roots and Pulse, to eat; spin and weave Cotton, and fasten together the large Feathers of Fowls, to cover their Nakedness; many of whom, in much Simplicity, live inoffensive in their Cottages, and take great Comfort in raising up Children.

Should we contemplate on their Circumstances, when suddenly attacked, and labour to understand their inexpressible Anguish of Soul, who survive the Conflict; should we think on inoffensive Women, who fled at the Alarm, and at their Return saw that Village, in which they and their Acquaintance were raised up, and had pleasantly spent their youthful Days, now lying in a gloomy Desolation; some shocked at finding the mangled Bodies of their near Friends amongst the Slain; others bemoaning the Absence of a Brother, a Sister, a Child, or a whole Family of Children, who, by cruel Men, are bound and carried to Market, to be sold, without the least Hopes of seeing them again: Add to this, the afflicted Condition of these poor Captives, who are separated from Family Connections, and all the Comforts arising from Friendship and Acquaintance, carried amongst a People of a strange Language, to be parted from their Fellow Captives, put to Labour in a Manner more servile and wearisome than what they were used to, with many sorrowful Circumstances attending their Slavery; and we must necessarily see, that it belongs not to the Followers of CHRIST to be Parties in such a Trade, on the Motives of outward Gain.

Though there were Wars and Desolations among the *Negroes*, before the *Europeans* began to trade there for Slaves, yet now the Calamities are greatly increased, so many Thousands being annually brought from thence; and we, by purchasing them, with Views of Self-interest, are become Parties with them, and accessary to that Increase.

In this Case, we are not joining against an Enemy who is fomenting Discords on our Continent, and using all possible Means to make Slaves of us and our Children; but against a People who have not injured us.

If those who were spoiled and wronged, should at length make Slaves of their Oppressors, and continue Slavery to their Posterity, it would look rigorous to candid Men: But to act that Part toward a People, when neither they nor their Fathers have injured us, hath something in it extraordinary, and requires our serious Attention.

Our Children breaking a Bone; getting so bruised, that a Leg or an Arm must be taken off; lost for a few Hours, so that we despair of their being found again; a Friend hurt, so that he dieth in a Day or two; these move us with Grief: And did we attend to these Scenes in *Africa*, in like Manner as if they were

75

transacted in our Presence; and sympathise with the *Negroes*, in all their Afflictions and Miseries, as we do with our Children or Friends; we should be more careful to do nothing in any Degree helping forward a Trade productive of so many, and so great Calamities. Great Distance makes nothing in our Favour.—To willingly join with Unrighteousness, to the Injury of Men who live some Thousand Miles off, is the same in Substance, as joining with it to the Injury of our Neighbours.

In the Eye of pure Justice, Actions are regarded according to the Spirit and Disposition they arise from: Some Evils are accounted scandalous, and the Desire of Reputation may keep selfish Men from appearing openly in them; but he who is shy on that Account, and yet by indirect Means promotes that Evil, and shares in the Profit of it, cannot be innocent.

He who, with View to Self-interest, buys a Slave, made so by Violence, and only on the Strength of such Purchase holds him a Slave, thereby joins Hands with those who committed that Violence, and in the Nature of Things becomes chargeable with the Guilt.

Suppose a Man wants a Slave, and being in *Guiney*, goes and hides by the Path where Boys pass from one little Town to another, and there catches one the

Day he expects to sail; and taking him on board, brings him home, without any aggravating Circumstances. Suppose another buys a Man, taken by them who live by Plunder and the Slave-Trade: They often steal them privately, and often shed much Blood in getting them. He who buys the Slave thus taken, pays those Men for their Wickedness, and makes himself Party with them.

Whatever Nicety of Distinction there may be, betwixt going in Person on Expeditions to catch Slaves, and buying those, with a View to Self-interest, which others have taken; it is clear and plain to an upright Mind, that such Distinction is in Words, not in Substance; for the Parties are concerned in the same Work, and have a necessary Connection with, and Dependance on, each other; for were there none to purchase Slaves, they who live by stealing and selling them, would of Consequence do less at it.

Some would buy a *Negroe* brought from *Guiney*, with a View to Self-interest, and keep him a Slave, who yet would seem to scruple to take Arms, and join with Men employed in taking Slaves.

Others have civil *Negroes*, who were born in our Country, capable and likely to manage well for themselves; whom they keep as Slaves, without ever trying them with Freedom, and take the Profit of their Labour as a Part of their Estates, and yet disapprove bringing them from their own Country.

If those *Negroes* had come here, as Merchants, with their Ivory and Gold Dust, in order to trade with us, and some powerful Person had took their Effects to himself, and then put them to hard Labour, and ever after considered them as Slaves, the Action would be looked upon as unrighteous.

Those *Negroe* Merchants having Children after their being among us, whose Endowments and Conduct were like other Peoples in common, who attaining to mature Age, and requesting to have their Liberty, should be told they were born in Slavery, and were lawful Slaves, and therefore their Request denied; the Conduct of such Persons toward them, would be looked upon as unfair and oppressive.

In the present Case, relating to Home-born *Negroes*, whose Understandings and Behaviour are as good as common among other People, if we have any Claim to them as Slaves, that Claim is grounded on their being the Children or Offspring of Slaves, who, in general, were made such through Means as unrighteous, and attended with more terrible Circumstances than the Case here supposed; so that when we trace our Claim to the Bottom, these Home-born *Negroes* having paid for their Education, and given reasonable Security to those who owned them, in case of their becoming chargeable, we have no more equitable Right to their Service, than we should if they were the Children of honest Merchants who came from *Guiney* in an *English* Vessel to trade with us.

If we claim any Right to them as the Children of Slaves, we build on the Foundation laid by them, who made Slaves of their Ancestors; so that of Necessity we must either justify the Trade, or relinquish our Right to them, as being the Children of Slaves.

Why should it seem right to honest Men to make Advantage by these People more than by others? Others enjoy Freedom, receive Wages, equal to their Work, at, or near, such Time as they have discharged these equitable Obligations they are under to those who educated them.—These have made no Contract to serve; been no more expensive in raising up than others, and many of them appear as likely to make a right Use of Freedom as other People; which Way then can an honest Man withhold from them that Liberty, which is the free Gift of the Most High to his rational Creatures?

The Upright in Heart cannot succeed the Wicked in their Wickedness; nor is it consonant to the Life they live, to hold fast an Advantage unjustly gained.

The *Negroes* who live by Plunder, and the

Slave-Trade, steal poor innocent Children, invade their Neighbours Territories, and spill much Blood to get these Slaves: And can it be possible for an honest Man to think that, with View to Self-interest, we may continue Slavery to the Offspring of these unhappy Sufferers, merely because they are the Children of Slaves, and not have a Share of this Guilt.

It is granted by many, that the Means used in getting them are unrighteous, and that buying them, when brought here, is wrong; yet as setting them free is attended with some Difficulty, they do not comply with it; but seem to be of the Opinion, that to give them Food and Raiment, and keep them Servants, without any other Wages, is the best Way to manage them that they know of: And hoping that their Children after them will not be cruel to the *Negroes*, conclude to leave them as Slaves to their Children.

While present outward Interest is the chief Object of our Attention, we shall feel many Objections in our Minds against renouncing our Claim to them, as the Children of Slaves; for being prepossessed with wrong Opinions, prevents our seeing Things clearly, which, to indifferent Persons, are easy to be seen.

Suppose a Person Seventy Years past, in low Circumstances, bought a *Negroe* Man and Woman, and that the Children of such Person are now wealthy, and have the Children of such Slaves. Admit that the first *Negroe* Man and his Wife did as much Business as their Master and Mistress, and that the Children of the Slaves have done some more than their young Masters: Suppose, on the whole, that the Expence of Living has been less on the *Negroes* Side, than on the other [all which are no improbable Suppositions] it follows, that in Equity these *Negroes* have a Right to a Part of this Increase; that should some Difficulties arise on their being set free, there is Reason for us patiently to labour through them.

As the Conduct of Men varies, relating to Civil Society; so different Treatment is justly due to them. Indiscreet Men occasion Trouble in the World; and it remains to be the Care of such, who seek the Good of Mankind, to admonish as they find Occasion.

The Slothfulness of some of them, in providing for themselves and Families, it is likely, would require the Notice of their Neighbours; nor is it unlikely that some would, with Justice, be made Servants, and others punished for their Crimes. Pure Justice points out to each Individual their Due; but to deny a People the Privilege of human Creatures, on a Supposition that, being free, many of them would be troublesome to us, is to mix the

Condition of good and bad Men together, and treat the whole as the worst of them deserve.

If we seriously consider, that Liberty is the Right of innocent Men; that the Mighty GOD is a Refuge for the Oppressed; that in Reality we are indebted to them; that they being set free, are still liable to the Penalties of our Laws, and as likely to have Punishment for their Crimes as other People: This may answer all our Objections. And to retain them in perpetual Servitude, without just Cause for it, will produce Effects, in the Event, more grievous than setting them free would do, when a real Love to Truth and Equity was the Motive to it.

Our Authority over them stands originally in a Purchase made from those who, as to the general, obtained theirs by Unrighteousness. Whenever we have Recourse to such Authority, it tends more or less to obstruct the Channels, through which the perfect Plant in us receives Nourishment.

There is a Principle, which is pure, placed in the human Mind, which in different Places and Ages hath had different Names; it is, however, pure, and proceeds from GOD.—It is deep, and inward, confined to no Forms of Religion, nor excluded from any, where the Heart stands in perfect Sincerity. In whomsoever this takes Root, and grows, of what Nation soever, they become Brethren, in the best

Sense of the Expression. Using ourselves to take Ways which appear most easy to us, when inconsistent with that Purity which is without Beginning, we thereby set up a Government of our own, and deny Obedience to him, whose Service is true Liberty.

He that has a Servant, made so wrongfully, and knows it to be so, when he treats him otherwise than a free Man, when he reaps the Benefit of his Labour, without paying him such Wages as are reasonably due to free Men for the like Service, Cloaths excepted; these Things, tho' done in Calmness, without any Shew of Disorder, do yet deprave the Mind in like Manner, and with as great Certainty, as prevailing Cold congeals Water. These Steps taken by Masters, and their Conduct striking the Minds of their Children, whilst young, leave less Room for that which is good to work upon them. The Customs of their Parents, their Neighbours, and the People with whom they converse, working upon their Minds; and they, from thence, conceiving Ideas of Things, and Modes of Conduct, the Entrance into their Hearts becomes, in a great Measure, shut up against the gentle Movings of uncreated Purity.

From one Age to another, the Gloom grows thicker and darker, till Error gets established by general Opinion; that whoever attends to perfect Goodness, and remains under the melting Influence of it, finds a Path unknown to many, and sees the Necessity to lean upon the Arm of Divine Strength, and dwell alone, or with a few, in the right committing their Cause to him, who is a Refuge for his People, in all their Troubles.

Where, through the Agreement of a Multitude, some Channels of Justice are stopped, and Men may support their Characters as just Men, by being just to a Party, there is great Danger of contracting an Alliance with that Spirit, which stands in Opposition to the GOD of Love, and spreads Discord, Trouble and Vexation among such who give up to the Influence of it.

Negroes are our Fellow Creatures, and their present Condition amongst us requires our serious Consideration. We know not the Time when those Scales, in which Mountains are weighed, may turn. The Parent of Mankind is gracious: His Care is over his smallest Creatures; and a Multitude of Men escape not his Notice: And though many of them are trodden down, and despised, yet he remembers them: He seeth their Affliction, and looketh upon the spreading increasing Exaltation of the Oppressor. He turns the Channels of Power, humbles the most haughty People, and gives Deliverance to the Oppressed, at such Periods as are consistent with his infinite Justice and Goodness. And wherever Gain is preferred to Equity, and wrong Things publickly encouraged to that Degree, that Wickedness takes Root, and spreads wide amongst the Inhabitants of a Country, there is real Cause for Sorrow to all such, whose Love to Mankind stands on a true Principle, and wisely consider the End and Event of Things.

FINIS

AN AFTERWORD ON WOOLMAN & SLAVERY

In 1746 John Woolman of Mount Holly, West Jersey, traveled on a religious mission through the colonies of Maryland, Virginia, and North Carolina. Everywhere he found Friends holding slaves, and when they lived easily on the slaves' labor, he felt "uneasy." On the whole, slavery appeared to him "as a dark gloominess hanging over the Land."[1] After his return, he sat down and wrote an essay in which he set forth *Some Considerations on the Keeping of Negroes,* and then he waited eight years before doing anything about its publication.

In 1750 his father lay on his deathbed. He was one of the first to know what his son had written, for Woolman had allowed his family to read his essay. The dying man urged him to have it published. Four years later, Woolman offered it to the Overseers of the Press of the Meeting for Sufferings (the executive body) of Philadelphia Yearly Meeting of Friends. They made a few alterations in it with Woolman's consent, and ordered it to be published and distributed among Friends. It was Woolman's first venture into print.

As time went on, the religious concern against slavery deepened with Woolman. Finally, towards 1760, he wrote a second and longer essay, *Considerations on Keeping Negroes . . . Part Second.* The Overseers of the Press approved, offering to print it at the Yearly Meeting's expense and give copies away. This plan did not satisfy Woolman. The funds of the Yearly Meeting had been provided by its members, many of whom were slaveholders. Woolman could see that these members would not be pleased to have an essay against slavery published at their expense and copies given away. "But as they who make a purchase buy that which they have a mind for," wrote Woolman, "I was easie to sell them, Expecting by that means they would more generaly be read with Attention."[2] He then gave the manuscript to Benjamin Franklin and David Hall to be printed. The price was set very low—only high enough to pay the cost of printing and binding. He sent some copies off to Friends in New York and Newport, Rhode Island, and kept some himself to give away "where there appear'd a prospect of doing it to advantage."[3]

Friends had for years been uneasy about the holding of Negroes in slavery. As early as 1657, George Fox, the founder of Quakerism, had written an epistle to "Friends beyond Sea that Have Blacks and Indians Slaves." He pointed out to them that God made all nations of one blood and that His gospel should be preached to all, including those in captivity. In 1671, after he had seen slaves laboring for Friends on Barbados, he urged that they be set free after a limited number of years and rewarded for their labors.[4] In 1688, a group of four Rhineland Friends at Germantown in Pennsylvania wrote out their objections to slavery and presented them to their Monthly, Quarterly, and Yearly Meetings. No official action was taken, but they had raised a question that would not cease to perplex Friends until the problem was solved. As time went on, individual Friends here and there in the American colonies raised questions about the morality of slavery. William Southeby, Cadwalader Morgan, Robert Pyle, John Hepburn, William Burling, Elihu Coleman, Ralph Sandiford, Benjamin Lay—these are the names of Friends who with greater or less clarity found themselves opposed on principle to slaveholding and took what seemed to them appropriate action to express their concerns. In no case did their meetings take strong action against slavery.[5]

It remained for John Woolman to serve as the herald who would really waken the conscience of the Society of Friends in America on the subject of slavery. Woolman was born in 1720 in a large Quaker family near Mount Holly on Rancocas Creek. Raised on his father's farm, at the age of twenty he went to work as a tailor and shopkeeper and conveyancer. The earliest inkling of his concern against slavery appeared in his *Journal* for the year 1743. One day, his employer asked him to write out a bill of sale for a slave girl. Woolman had not thought much about slavery hitherto, but suddenly, when asked to take some part in it, he was appalled by the wickedness of the practice. He remembered, however, that he was employed by the man who asked him to do it and that the buyer was a respectable old Friend. So, although he did as he was told, he did say before his employer and the buyer that he thought slavekeeping inconsistent with Christianity. Later, he always thought he should have asked to be "Excused from it, as a thing against conscience, for such it was."[6]

Not long after, a young Friend who had taken a Negro into his house asked Woolman to write out an instrument of slavery for him. Woolman promptly said he was "not easie to write it," because he believed the practice "was not right."[7] Henceforth he steadily declined to write wills or bills of sale involving slaves. He could see by now that "acting contrary to present outward interest, from a motive of Divine love and in regard to Truth and Righteousness, and thereby incuring the resentments of people, opens the way to a treasure which is better than silver, and to a friendship Exceeding the friendship of men."[8]

The problem of slavery was constantly on Woolman's mind in these days. In 1753 he composed an epistle on slavery which the Yearly Meeting of that year agreed to send to Friends in Virginia. When Philadelphia Yearly Meeting assembled in 1754, it decided to send that epistle to all Friends in America. *Some Considertions on the Keeping of Negroes* had just been published; Woolman included in the epistle several passages from the essay. Thus his ideas reached Friends in all parts of the American colonial world.

His ideas were advanced in such a way as to appeal to nearly all Friends, including even some who held slaves. "To conclude, 'Tis a Truth most certain," he wrote at the close of the first essay, "that a Life guided by Wisdom from above, agreeable with Justice, Equity, and Mercy, is throughout consistent and amiable, and truly beneficial to Society; the Serenity and Calmness of Mind in it, affords an unparallel'd Comfort in this Life, and the End of it is blessed."[9] In other words, he was appealing to his readers to be faithful Friends, to follow the Inward Light: "my Inclination is to persuade, and intreat, and simply give Hints of my Way of Thinking."[10] What Christian and particularly what Quaker who held slaves could read his words and fail to feel a qualm of conscience about his use of slaves?

He used a good many quotations from the Bible, which, like many other reformers, he found to be full of angry passages that strengthened his case. In particular, he could quote the Hebrew prophets who constantly condemned the Jewish people for buying and keeping slaves. The tone is always religious, but nonetheless earnest for all that. Wherever one dips into these pages, one finds the same degree of calmness, of serenity, but also the determination that is everywhere in Woolman's writing. He always looks within himself to find the truth, for as a good Friend he believed that God would reveal it through the Light Within.

Basically, what he says is quite simple—that the Golden Rule applies equally to all men, no matter what their color. Thus no man could be rightly held in servitude and no man could be happy on earth who did not favor setting the enslaved Negroes free. If our natures were "so far renewed, that to exercise Righteousness and Loving Kindness . . . towards all Men, without Respect of Persons, is easy to us, or is our Delight . . . there is a good Foundation to Hope, that the Blessing of God will sweeten our Treasures during our Stay in this Life, and our Memory be savory, when we are entered into Rest."[11] His essays, like his epistles, were designed to be read by individual Friends as part of their religious duty. Any reader who was a good Quaker would, upon reading what he had written, hold up his own relationship with Negroes to the scrutiny of his Inner Light and take the action that was set before him. Quaker books, pamphlets, and epistles were read chiefly to guide the Inner Light, or rather to guide the Friend in interpreting its messages. At writing such words, John Woolman was very good indeed, for he as much as any Friend was one who followed every genuine "leading" he had from within.

Woolman wrote considerably more than his *Journal* and the essays here reprinted. The essays appeared many times later, usually in connection with the reprinting of his *Journal* or as part of his collected *Works*. It is worth noting that the first essay was reprinted twelve times, the second ten times, between 1800 and 1860— clearly a part of the pre-Civil War antislavery propaganda effort.

Woolman's aim in writing was always to be simple and clear. He achieved this goal best in his *Journal*, but one can see him struggling for it in his other works. Look, for example, at the opening paragraph of the first essay or its final paragraph. In both it is perfectly clear what Woolman is saying, clear and emphatic. The use of long words would not increase either its clarity or its emphasis. Nor would the use of long, complicated sentences achieve the same end. Woolman unfailingly looked within himself, consulted the eternal wisdom that lay deep in his soul, and did his best to set down the words, the simple yet urgent message the Inward Light had given him. What he wrote could be read by Christians of every description. The slaveholders among them might not set their slaves free, but at least they knew what Woolman considered to be God's will for them, and how God was determined to punish them if they failed to do His will.

NOTES: 1. *The Journal and Essays of John Woolman*, ed. Amelia Mott Gummere (New York, 1922), 167; 2. *ibid.*, 244; 3. *idem;* 4. Thomas E. Drake, *Quakers and Slavery in America* (New Haven, 1950), 5; 5. *ibid.*, chapters I, II; 6. Woolman, *Journal*, 161; 7. *ibid.*, 161-2; 8. *ibid.*, 175; 9. 27-8; 10. 25; 11. 27.

FREDERICK B. TOLLES

*This facsimile of The Gehenna
Press limited edition was
printed to memorialize the bicenten-
nial of John Woolman's death in 1772.
The texts follow the first editions.
The portrait by Leonard Baskin is
based on a drawing from memory by
Robert Smith III. The types are
Centaur & Arrighi. The pressman
for the original edition was
Harold McGrath.*